Healthy Eating

Fruits

Nancy Dickmann

Heinemann Library
Chicago, Illinois

www.heinemannraintree.com
Visit our website to find out
more information about
Heinemann-Raintree books.

To order:
☎ Phone 888-454-2279
🖳 Visit www.heinemannraintree.com
to browse our catalog and order online.

Edited by Siân Smith, Nancy Dickmann, and Rebecca Rissman
Designed by Joanna Hinton-Malivoire
Picture research by Elizabeth Alexander
Production by Victoria Fitzgerald
Originated by Capstone Global Library Ltd
Printed and bound in China by South China Printing Company Ltd

ISBN 978-1-4329-3978-6
14 13 12 11 10
10 9 8 7 6 5 4 3 2 1

Library of Congress Cataloging-in-Publication Data
Dickmann, Nancy.
  Fruits / Nancy Dickmann.
    p. cm. -- (Healthy eating)
  Includes bibliographical references and index.
  ISBN 978-1-4329-3978-6 (hc) -- ISBN 978-1-4329-3985-4 (pb) 1. Fruit in
human nutrition--Juvenile literature. I. Title.
  QP144.F78D53 2011
  613.2--dc22
                    2009045461

Acknowledgements
We would like to thank the following for permission to reproduce
photographs: © Capstone Publishers p.**22** (Karon Dubke); Alamy p.**11** (©
Bloom Works Inc.); Getty Images pp.**8** (Rosemary Calvert/Photographer's
Choice), **17** (Alistair Berg/Digital Vision), **20**, **23 middle** (Heinrich van
den Berg/Gallo Images); iStockphoto pp.**5**, **7** (© Elena Korenbaum), **13**
(© Suprijono Suharjoto), **23 top** (© Mark Hatfield); Photolibrary pp. **9**, **13**
(John Smith/Fancy), **10** (Pixtal Images), **14** (Medicimage), **15** (PureStock),
16 (Radius Images), **21** (Willy De L'Horme/Photononstop); Shutterstock
pp.**4** (© Denis and Yulia Pogostins), **6** (© Georgios Alexandris), **12** (©
Simone van den Berg), **18** (© Monkey Business Images); USDA Center for
Nutrition Policy and Promotion p.**19**.

Front cover photograph of fruit reproduced with permission of © Capstone
Publishers (Karon Dubke). Back cover photograph reproduced with
permission of iStockphoto (© Suprijono Suharjoto).

We would like to thank Dr Sarah Schenker for her invaluable help in the
preparation of this book.

Every effort has been made to contact copyright holders of material
reproduced in this book. Any omissions will be rectified in subsequent
printings if notice is given to the publishers.

Contents

What Are Fruits?

Fruits are parts of plants.

Eating fruits can keep us healthy.

orange

Some fruits grow on trees.

vine

grapes

Some fruits grow on vines.

Looking at Fruits

orange

Many fruits are round.

Fruits can be many different colors.

grapes

raisins

We dry some fruits. Raisins are dried grapes.

We make juice from some fruits.

How Fruits Help Us

Fruits are full of nutrients.

You need nutrients to stay healthy.

Eating bananas keeps your blood healthy.

Eating kiwis helps you fight colds.

Eating fruits helps your body
make energy.

You need energy to work
and play.

Healthy Eating

We need to eat five servings of fruit and vegetables each day.

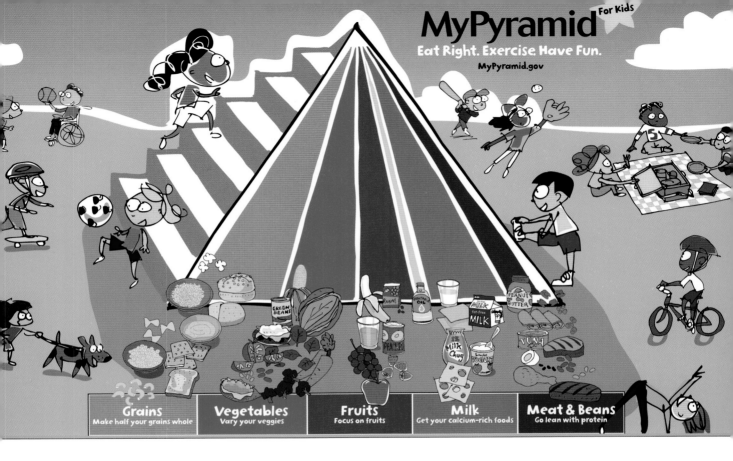

The food pyramid tells us to eat foods from each food group.

Staying Healthy

We eat fruits to stay healthy.

We eat fruits because they taste good!

Find the Fruits

Here is a healthy breakfast.

Can you find the fruits?

Answer on page 24

Picture Glossary

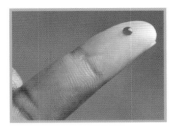 **blood** red liquid inside your body. Blood takes food and air to all your body parts.

 **energy** the power to do something. We need energy when we work or play.

 **nutrients** things our bodies need to stay healthy. You can get nutrients in different foods.

Index

Answer to quiz on page 22: The fruits include the strawberries in the bowl, and the oranges that have been made into orange juice in the glass.

Notes for parents and teachers

Before reading

Explain that we need to eat a range of different foods to stay healthy. Splitting foods into different groups can help us understand how much food we should eat from each group. Introduce the fruits group. How many different fruits can children think of? Explain that eating at least five portions of fruits and vegetables every day can help us to stay healthy.

After reading

• Play "Guess the mystery fruit." Place a fruit or fruit picture into a bag. Alternatively, choose a fruit from the cover of this book. Give the children clues to help them identify the fruit. For example, "It has seeds. It tastes sour. It grows on a tree." Take turns describing different fruits.

• Ask children to bring in some fruits. These could be their favorite fruits or fruits they have never tried before. Share the fruits with the class. Explain that our taste buds change and why it is good to try new things. Create a pictogram to show the class's favorite fruits.

• Ask children to sit in a circle with one child standing in the center. Choose four different fruits and give one fruit name to each child. When the child in the center calls out a fruit, everyone with that fruit name should swap places. The child in the center should try to find a place to sit. The caller can also choose to call out "fruit salad." If they do so, everyone in the circle needs to swap places.